P9-EDP-080

Cat Psychology

R.H. Smythe

Frontispiece: An ordinary domesticated cat.

ISBN 0-87666-854-6

Distributed in the U.S. by T.F.H. Publications, Inc., 211 West Sylvania Avenue, P.O. Box 427, Neptune, N.J. 07753; in England by T.F.H. (Gt. Britain) Ltd., 13 Nutley Lane, Reigate, Surrey; in Canada to the book store and library trade by Clarke, Irwin & Company, Clarwin House, 791 St. Clair Avenue West, Toronto 10, Ontario; in Canada to the pet trade by Rolf C. Hagen Ltd., 3225 Sartelon Street, Montreal 382, Quebec; in Southeast Asia by Y.W. Ong, 9 Lorong 36 Geylang, Singapore 14; in Australia and the South Pacific by Pet Imports Pty. Ltd., P.O. Box 149, Brookvale 2100, N.S.W., Australia; in South Africa by Valiant Publishers (Pty.) Ltd., P.O. Box 78236, Sandton City, 2146, South Africa; Published by T.F.H. Publications, Inc., Ltd., The British Crown Colony of Hong Kong.

Contents

Introduction

Despite the fact that modern psychologists claim that man is the only living animal possessing a brain capable of constructive thought, they overlook the fact that the cat, in one form or another, existed—flourished, in fact—on this earth many millions of years before man put in an appearance in his present form.

Whatever may have happened in the Garden of Eden, it is quite likely that the cat, from some hidden corner, could have been an interested spectator, wondering, perhaps, what manner of creature was about to make its appearance, and, above all, whether the specimen might be good to eat.

It must be taken into account that even if the modern cats were originally descended from the sabre-toothed tiger or some other member of the early felines, domestic types have never been called upon to make any drastic changes in their appearance. There have been changes, yes, but no *drastic* changes.

This leads one to believe that today's cats' prototypes must have been constructed on very sound foundations and that the pattern, perfected through the ages, must by now be very close to the ideal.

The cat first came into being with a complete armory of teeth and claws, plus a remarkable agility, all of which rendered it capable not only of procuring its own food but also of defending itself against all comers!

Man-to-be descended or ascended—however one likes to regard it—from an entirely different prototype. He has had

Portrait of a common "tabby" cat. Tabby markings are also the markings or pattern of the "original" cat. When present in other breeds for which the standard doesn't allow tabby markings, such markings are considered as faults.

to lose his tail, learn to stand erect, grow a far larger brain, and discover, through the ages, how to dominate the world around him.

But he has never really learned to dominate the cat, one of the few animals who can disregard man completely or live in close association with him, whichever is more pleasing to the cat!

The cat joined forces with man about 2,000 B.C., probably in Egypt, and then considered whether or not to share a home with him.

A young bobcat in captivity. Bobcats are useful to the American farmer because they help keep the rodent population down. They are hunted for their fur, and the meat is eaten sometimes. Some individuals, but not very many, can become tame. Photo by L. van der Meid.

The chief character of a Persian cat is the long and silky fur. Short ears, short legs, and a short tail are a few of the standard characters required for showing Persians. Photo by Mrs. John Bloem.

The association between the two became stable in the case of human tribes who had fixed abodes and some idea, however primitive, of gracious living. (Cats have never attached themselves to nomadic races.)

Where there were men—an untidy race—so there were vermin, which provided both food and enjoyable hunting, a factor making man's domain more appealing to his new-found aquaintance. And when man found that this new companion was capable of ridding his sleeping quarters of rats, snakes, and other unwelcome visitors, the bond, on man's side, at least, became complete and lasting.

As a result of this human interest in cats and the study of cat types which thrive best in domestication, a great many

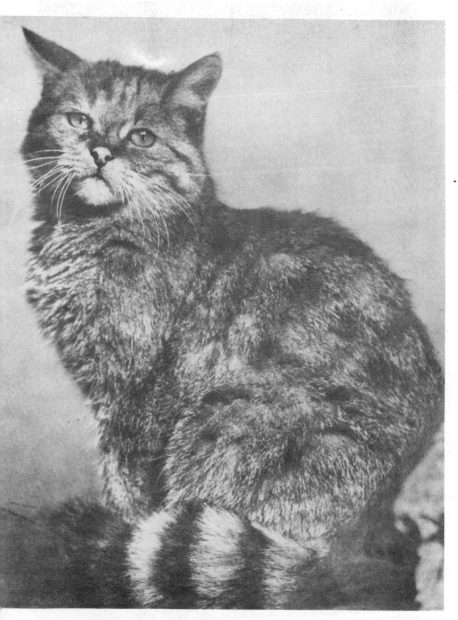

The tabby color pattern originated as an adaptive coloration in wild cats. It is one of the characters which persist in domestic cats that are without pedigrees. Photo by Staneck.

The Siamese cat breed was first introduced into the United States almost a century ago. The presumption that this popular breed originated in Thailand (formerly Siam) is not generally doubted.

distinct varieties have been established. Their distribution has become so extensive that the domestic cat, numerically, has become the greatest among all the Felidae.

But not all of our domestic cats owe their origin to the same line of ancestry. So many attempts have been made to acquire and domesticate kittens from a wide range of wild

The Abyssinian is another breed of short-haired cat. The Abyssinian is sometimes called the "rabbit" cat on account of the hare-like fur. Photo by L. van der Meid.

stocks—derived from a great many different countries—that we now find at every cat show throughout the country a number of varieties very unlike our conception of the domestic cat. In some cases we would be hard put to name each breed or its country of origin without referring to the catalogue.

Many of these breeds have their own peculiar mental characteristics. Some are docile and affectionate; others are disdainful. Some forget constantly to sheathe their claws,

The Burmese, less well known than the Siamese, looks like the Siamese, but it has darker fur and orange eyes instead of blue. Photo by W. Chandoha.

The curly condition of the fur first appeared in domestic cats as a mutation. By selection and breeding this character is now fixed in some breeds like the curly-coated Rex cat shown here. Photo by Mrs. W. Weiss.

and others, a very few, need careful handling and are not bursting with affection.

The association between man and cat, through countless centuries, has probably been responsible for the feline's existence in so many different climes.

The ancient Romans owned cats, but these cats did not spread generally throughout Europe until the early Christian days. They were present in numbers in India from 200 B.C. and in China from 400 B.C.

The Egyptians, in order to increase the number of cats in their own country, collected cats from various parts of Africa. It is probable that these non-native cats mated with

Although the cheetah is the fastest running mammal known, it is an endangered species. The original larger range of the cheetah has been greatly diminished by changing environment, reduced prey, and demand for the beautifully patterned fur.

It will be unusual if a kitten refrains from "playing" with anything that moves, such as a mouse or a toy. In the wild the playing ritual leads to hunting behavior that is indispensable to survival. A Three Lions photo.

the indigenous cats living in the area to which they were taken. The mates were principally desert cats.

The Phoenicians caught cats from Africa and the coasts of the Mediterranean and brought them to Cornwall in exchange for tin and copper. On other occasions they introduced cats into Rome and Japan.

In Egypt, the cat was an object of worship, and any evidence of ill-treatment was a punishable offence.

On the other hand, in so-called Christian Europe, cats

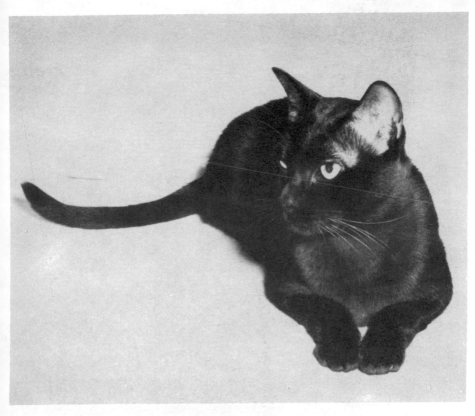

A sleek and shiny fur together with a pair of glowing eyes all add to the mysterious appeal of black cats. Photo by H. Dyott.

were regarded as creatures of evil portent. The public burning of cats as a method of abolishing evil forebodings was a common occurrence.

It was not long before cats in Italy became objects of worship and adoration. Their new owners developed the belief that the fire in their eyes denoted the presence of a sun existing within their brains.

The cult of the cat, and its worship, became so annoying to the Church of Rome that Pope Innocent VIII instituted an inquisition and brought in alleged cat worshippers for trial. The guilty were burned at the stake.

Black-cat cults and superstitions still exist in some parts of the world, including highly civilized countries. Photo by R. Larson.

As compared with the dog, which shares our homes with domestic cats, the latter show far less anatomical diversities. Beneath the skin all cats are more or less alike, whereas dogs, by virtue of various mutations intentionally fixed by breeders, vary to such an extent that it sometimes is hard to believe they are all members of the same species.

Cat bones that littered the floors of some of the caves at one time inhabited by man have only recently been discovered. This does not necessarily indicate any mutually friendly association between cat and man at that time, for it is pos-

Shown is a dramatic comparison between a Great Dane and a Chihuahua. On the contrary, differences among cat breeds are not too spectacular. A Three Lions photo.

Though their type and beginnings are different (the Siamese is a natural breed and the Rex is a mutation) what these two breeds of cat share in common with most other domestic felines is their mutual curiousity.

sible that prehistoric man had no scruples regarding his choice of a meat dish. One cannot overlook the possibility that the cats from which these bones came may have served a dual purpose and that the conditions under which human beings lived in those days might have favored a birth rate among cats over and above the number required for the destruction of vermin.

19

The cats of long ago were probably independent creatures, willing to share lodgings with another being for as long as they could obtain sufficient food, combined with a degree of protection against the elements, as well as against other animals with a liking for feline flesh. They still are.

Throughout the ages, cats have had a deserved reputation for being able to take care of themselves. Almost without exception they seem to come out on top.

Nevertheless, man has a great deal to offer the cat, and the cat may well retain our deepest respect, even despite—or

In spite of the independent nature of cats, some individuals are willing to share the comforts of home with other animals. Photo by L. van der Meid.

The ability to act quickly is not lost even among highly domesticated breeds. This Siamese cat is just as quick in getting hold of a toy as its cousin in the wilds in catching prey. Photo by L. van der Meid.

perhaps because of—the fact that it appreciates luxury and prefers a well-padded sofa to a pile of stones. Many of us would do the same.

The original wild cat, contrary to general belief, was not the ancestor of our present domestic cat. The wild cat was common throughout Britain and Scotland until the early part of the nineteenth century. Its disappearance was largely due to the fact that the skins of both rabbits and wild cats were the cheapest obtainable in the days when fur clothing was very much in vogue. Wild cats were hunted in the royal

Whiskers are very important sensory organs of all cats. Removing them will certainly affect a cat's behavior. A Three Lions photo.

At present it is a crime to import, sell and trade pelts of several endangered feline species.

forests and practically exterminated from the areas where they thrived the best. In some parts of Scotland, notably in the Highlands, the wild cats may still be found, living mainly among rocks.

The wild cat and the domestic cat seldom breed together, partly because of the difference in their structural characteristics. The male wild cat, in spite of its short tail, may often measure thirty-eight inches in length. Kittening, when the sire is a wild cat, may be fraught with difficulty, as the head of a wild cat kitten is comparatively larger and wider across than the head of a domestic kitten. It also is inclined to be rather square in shape.

Also, the wild cat carries a large number of very stiff whiskers. The body is thick and very muscular, a yellowish-

Some domestic cats will chase and kill birds, but they rarely eat them. In the wild, however, predation is a necessity for survival. Photo by L. van der Meid.

grey in color, covered with broad black stripes, and one wide stripe down the spine. Wild cats are solitary animals, meeting others only during the mating season. They are vicious and unpredictable; if cornered, they will attack.

They live mainly on rats, rabbits, field mice and bank voles; and also birds, if they can catch them, which they attempt to do by stalking them and then suddenly springing off the ground in order to grab them in mid-air. Wild cats are not adverse to newly-born lambs or a fawn either.

We have one authentic account of a domesticated female cat's having mated with a wild cat. One of the resulting kittens, in a half-starved condition, was rescued by a local family but eventually left them. It did not appear able, however, to support itself, and it became emaciated. Eventually a lady living nearby enticed it into her house with milk. She fed it for several weeks with a spoon, on egg custard and mashed fish. The cat finally recovered and died at the age of fifteen years.

During its lifetime, this cat was exceptionally intelligent and good-natured. One of its many tricks was to stay out late at night and then, after everyone had gone to bed, make repeated jumps up the backdoor of the house, lift the iron knocker and let it fall. It would continue to do this until someone came down to let it in.

In Britain, cats are still wild animals by law, being regard-

This cat is presumably ringing the doorbell to summon persons inside to open the door. Cats normally scratch doors to attract attention whenever they want to get in or out.

The privilege of keeping in your home a wild cat like the bobcat seen here entails much responsibility on the part of the keeper. One should be cognizant of the possible dangers: injuries from bites and scratches, and possible diseases such as rabies, parasites, etc.

A pair of jaguarundi cubs. This small cat species occurs only in the New World, from South America to the southern United States.

ed as uncontrollable. For example, if one's dog killed a lamb, the owner would be held responsible. If a cat killed a brood of chickens, though, its owner could not be called upon to pay for the loss.

Cats were almost absent in South America before the Panama land bridges connecting North and South America were rebuilt during the Pleistocene Period. Only the puma represented the cat family in both North and South America. In the United States the puma is referred to (among other things) as the mountain lion, cougar, painter and catamount. The jaguar, puma, jaguarundi and a few other members of the Felidae belong exclusively to the New World. They are quite distinct from the cats of the Old World, and the only member common to both is the lynx.

A margay exercising in the park. Except for their smaller size and relatively longer tail, margays look very much like ocelots.

Scratching is a feline habit shared by all kinds of cats, big or small, wild or domesticated. A Three Lions photo.

The continent with the highest cat population is Asia. The West Indies, Madagascar, Australia, New Zealand and the Oceanic Islands are all entirely devoid of indigenous cats.

Cats have always been associated with superstitions and weird beliefs, mainly because they were never beholden to humanity. As a race, cats have always been able to live and multiply without having to seek assistance. In other words they could exist despite humanity, which is a sure way to attract human attention.

Witches were believed to carry the blood of cats mingled with their own, enabling the witch to take on, at will, the shape and appearance of a cat. In consequence, it was imagined that if one ill-treated a stray cat, or failed to succor it, or give it proper respect, the cat might have the power to cast a spell upon the offender.

Black cats have forever been thought to be harbingers of good or evil fortune, and in Cornwall when one met a black cat unexpectedly, one found it advisable to lick a finger and make a wet cross on the toecap of one's boot or shoe. To the contrary, in Cornwall, as well as Yorkshire, whenever fishing boats went to sea, a wife would keep a black cat—if it were obtainable—confined in her house until her husband's return. If the cat strayed or escaped while the master was at sea, the consequences might be disastrous!

I Kittens in the Wild

The homeless stray female cat usually produces two litters a year. She manages, as a rule, to raise a high percentage of her kittens to weaning age. After that her responsibility ceases. The kittens then reach the most precarious period of their existence.

The interesting feature is that even though the mother cat

The best inducement for any animal, including wild ones, to approach man is food. Young cats in particular will seldom refuse milk. Photo by L. van der Meid.

Cats and dogs can exist peacefully under the same roof. Cat-dog relationships are usually determined by early experience and training. Photo by L. van der Meid.

is comparatively tame and gentle, her kittens, born in the wild without any human contact, never become "imprinted," as Konrad Lorenz puts it.

Very simply stated, the "imprinting" theory holds that the first human being a young animal sees when its eyes open becomes a paternal or maternal figure. If the contact between the infant animal and the human figure persists, the loyalty on the part of the former will last throughout life.

When there is no imprinting, the young animals become extremely wild. By the time they are a month old, they attack, in their small way, any human being who may approach them. A four-inch scar on the forearm of the writer confirms such a happening, which might not be worth mentioning, had it not a sequel. This is the story:

32

Lioness (above) and male lion. Males have manes that tend to darken with age. The range of the lion in the past hundred years has been greatly reduced to such a degree that it is now found chiefly in national parks and reserves in Africa.

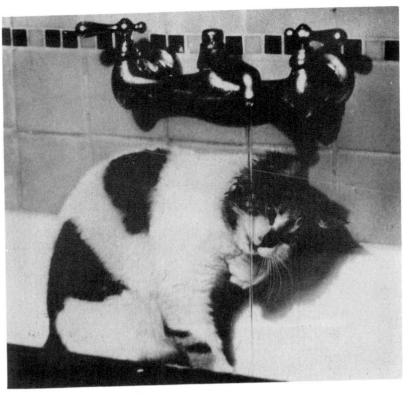
This cat is drinking water flowing from a tap just as it would from a trickle of water found in the woods. Photo by F. Dicke.

Two years ago a twelve-month-old black and white female cat made her appearance in the village where the writer lived. I discovered that she had a litter of kittens in the bed of a small stream; the kittens were under a small stone bridge, common in Cornwall. Although the site was dry and somewhat hidden when the kittens were born, a sudden thunderstorm with torrential rain soon created difficulties.

Mother Cat—as she has since been known—carried her four kittens one at a time by the scruff of the neck to a small tool shed at the bottom of the writer's garden. From then on her difficulties were almost over, because a worker laid down food at a suitable spot several times daily.

When a month old, the kittens would creep out for food, one or two at a time if they thought no other animal or human being was in sight, but they would bolt for safety if anyone appeared, even in the distance.

The kittens, though only one generation removed from domestication, were little *wild* animals. When I attempted to stroke one of them, it flew at me, jumped off the ground and severely lacerated my arm.

Not all of the hazards to the life of a cat are found outside the home. Loose or frayed electrical cords, for example, can electrocute a cat. Such tragedies happen. Photo by K. Donnelly.

Close-up of a sleeping lion cub. Cubs, unlike adults, are marked by well-defined spots which disappear with age. They also lack tufts in the tail.

Opposite:
A lioness carrying its young by the scruff of the neck. A litter of four cubs is normal in the wild, and the cubs will remain with the mother for almost two years.

A mother cat carrying one of her kittens by the scruff of the neck. It is not unusual for her to move the litter to different places in the house.

The interesting fact is that kittens born in the wilds and never "imprinted" by early contact with human parent figures seldom gain complete confidence in mankind.

We eventually adopted Mother Cat, and one of her male kittens, black and white, which now rejoices in the name "Charley." Both mother and son have been neutered.

Charley tolerates people and can even be lifted and fed for a little while, after which realisation overtakes him, and he will nip your hand or arm with his teeth, jump to the ground and bolt. In our kitchen we have a large dresser with lots of drawers. One small drawer is missing and this leaves a space leading into an empty cupboard. This represents Charley's bolt-hole. Being distrustful of people, he flies down the hole

Although one can carry a kitten like a mother cat would the kitten may not especially like this. It can turn rapidly and bite or scratch the handler. A Three Lions photo.

An Amur leopard, also known as long-haired Manchurian leopard. Leopards used to be found throughout Africa and Asia, but their range has been greatly reduced in the present century by hunting and increased demand for fur.

Opposite:
Among the cats, the hunting leopard or cheetah is the most differentiated species. The long legs, small head, and non-retractable claws are some of the characters adapted for hunting fast-moving prey like deer. In the past cheetahs were used by the nobility for hunting, just as dogs are used in modern times.

An ordinary paper bag can offer refuge from "intruders" for a shy or frightened cat, or the bag can be just a handy object to play with. Photo by N. McCormick.

out of sight the moment the coalman calls or the greengrocer's van stops outside.

The coalman calls on Monday and the greengrocer on Thursday. Charley appears to know the days of the week because on Monday and Thursday mornings, three hours before the tradesmen appear, Charley will be somewhere within easy reach of his bolt-hole.

As soon as they have called and left the area, Charley is himself again and will walk about the house and garden with impunity.

But he makes close friends with nobody, not even with persons in the habit of "dropping in." As soon as they ring the bell, he runs upstairs and stays under a bed until they leave. He is, however, a marvelous ratter and keeps the rodent population in this country village at a respectable level. Although the writer has been in close association with Charley since soon after his birth (and the two are excellent friends) I still cannot pick Charley up or even stroke him on the ground, not because he is vicious but simply because Charley is afraid of people. One might say that he has never lost his natural instinct for self-preservation, because he never went through the process of "imprinting."

Mother Cat, who probably underwent a normal kittenhood in domestication before she "went wild," or was dis-

Unfamiliar voices and faces can frighten some cats, especially a completely house-bound one. The space underneath an empty chair is usually a favorite "hiding" spot. Photo by K. Donnelly.

Snow leopards resemble true leopards in appearance and in having pupils that are round when contracted, but they are not capable of roaring—they purr instead. Systematists consider snow leopards as intermediate between small cats and big cats.

The black panther (right) is a melanistic form of leopard, just as we find the black cat as a melanistic type of domestic cat (below).

A toilet-trained cat just like the author's pet, Charley. Photo by L. van der Meid.

carded by her original owners, whichever it may have been, is a perfectly normal and sweet-natured cat, whose only bolthole is on the counterpane of her protector's bed!

This demonstrates how quickly a new generation of cats can suddenly lose all sense of the "civilization" acquired during the centuries they have lived in domestication.

One cannot help noticing that when rearing a litter of kittens they never come when called unless one stands with a saucer of food in one's hand.

Nor do they respond, later in life, to their names which have been given to them.

Being individuals appears to be a cult with cats. Under normal conditions they do not form social groups, even on farms, where a lot of cats enjoy semi-wild lives, and live on milk drunk from the pails at milking time and on the mice which they catch.

Litter boxes are necessities of modern living for house cats. They are inexpensive, sanitary, and very convenient. Photo by K. Donnelly.

The tiger is a powerful and massive predator from Asia, as the lion is from Africa. These two animals do not overlap in range, but they can hybridize in captivity. A Muller-Schmida photo.

Tiger cubs are striped like the adults but have lighter background coloration. In contrast to the leopard, melanism has not been observed in tigers; the contrary, however, partial albinism, has.

Opposite, lower photo:
Tigers are often found immersed in streams and are known to swim for several miles. Their main prey in river areas is water bucks. Tigers are almost invisible among the tall grasses as they wait for the prey along the banks. The body stripes blend very well with the background.

Pete, the cat pictured here, may habitually sit in the same spot behind the bars, but it would be uncommon for a domesticated cat to defend its territory as vigorously as a wild cat would. Territoriality is only slightly developed in domestic cats.

Fighting over food between cats is greatly minimized or avoided by simply providing cats, especially adults, with separate dishes. Photo by L. van der Meid.

The only place where cats congregate is in ancient buildings such as the Coliseum in Rome, where hundreds of cats get together for shelter, but still retain their individuality. The only reason for this is that there are, in many districts throughout the world, thousands of unwanted cats—another indication that cats make good mothers, even if their prolificacy is to be deplored.

The puma, cougar, or mountain lion is the most widely distributed cat of the Americas. The puma cub is strikingly patterned with irregular rows of black spots, while the adult is not. Pumas occur in various shades of gray or red. Reds predominate in tropical areas while the grays are found in dry areas.

The northern lynx is found in forested areas of Europe, Asia, and North America. Tufted ears and prominent side whiskers are some of its distinguishing features. Populations of this feline are on the decline because its fur is valuable.

II A Cat in the House

The homes of cats vary a great deal. Home may consist of one or two rooms with little opportunity for a cat to wander far away, or it may be a country house with acres of ground, or it might be anywhere between the two.

The fact is, however (and I have just had a personal opportunity to make a note of the fact) that the great majority of cats adapt themselves remarkably well and quickly to the conditions in which they find themselves.

The outdoor cat is usually in better condition, provided it has a good home, than the cat pampered indoors. The former keeps in a more fit condition and with luck, leads a longer life, provided, of course, that it escapes the dogs and foxes, the spring traps, the slug bait and rat poisons, as well as the organo-phosphorus sprays spread *anywhere, or everywhere,* by the farmers. Unfortunately, in a great many households the cat is almost completely ignored. Its job is to keep the mice away and that is all.

But in the hands of the cat lover, possession can be a joy (though also a responsibility), because most cats enjoy and need human society. Mother Cat and Charley, the writer's two cats referred to in Chapter One, have recently moved with me from a place in the country, where they enjoyed free range over the countryside, to a midland city. Apart from a back garden, walled-in and strewn with sand, they have no place in which to exercise and one would think they would miss the open farmland to which they had been accustomed.

However, and this is the point to which I wish to draw attention, the two cats have, in a matter of days, adapted themselves to circumstance. They risk their lives, whenever a window is left open even a little, by squeezing out onto the narrow windowsills where they sit sunning themselves with a twenty-foot drop beneath them. They go into the back garden, climb the walls and disappear into nowhere, returning later, ready for their next meal. They have adjusted their toilet arrangements very hygienically. Mother uses a large enamel bowl half-filled with newspaper, while Charley adjourns to the lavatory, props himself up on the seat and never makes a mistake. So far he has not attempted to pull the chain. The point is that in spite of their complete change of environment, both cats appear perfectly happy and contented.

All this would seem to prove that in the case of the domestic cat, territory is not freehold and unchangeable, and that the most important thing in life is to be with one's friends, enjoy a certain amount of comfortable living and be assured of plenty to eat and drink. Probably a sound piece of philosophy on the part of the cat.

In the ordinary course of events it might be expected that these two cats would adopt the usual practice of marking out their new territory. Seeing that both cats have been neutered, it may be presumed that they now lack the scented material for the job, though neither seems to even have any inclination to set about the task.

In the usual course of events male and female cats spray trees, shrubs, walls and other people's doorsteps with an augmented urine possessing a very rank odor. After this they rub their heads in the fluid and then rub them on other objects. It is uncertain as to why cats do this. The procedure appears to be more like leaving a visiting card than any desire to intimidate other cats in the neighbourhood.

Other cats approach the site, probably store the particular aroma in their memories, then add a little of their own urine

Two views of the serval, one of the smaller cats of Africa. Servals frequent grassy areas near streams where rodents, lizards and some birds are hunted.

The most striking characteristic of the caracal or desert lynx is its tufted ears. Caracals are mainly found in the dry areas of Africa, the Near East, and Central India.

Each cat has individual likes and dislikes. This tabby cat prefers open areas, whereas the white one insists on keeping to herself in cramped spaces. Photo by K. Donnelly.

on top of the original. In doing so, they show no signs of fear or awareness of a possible enemy. Territory marking by cats appears to be more in the nature of a social custom, based on politeness, then upon something in the nature of a deterrent.

The first thing the two cats did when being introduced to their new home was to wander from room by room, and it is remarkable how after only a few days they knew the geography of the premises, the whereabouts of every window, just how far it had been left open and whether it might be just possible to get through to the other side. I think the expression 'the other side,' is paramount in the vocabulary of every cat. Doors and windows must have another side, and the particular side at which the cat may be detained at any moment is, in every cat's opinion, the wrong one.

Sometimes Charley, the explorer, has been lucky in more senses than one. He found a bedroom window with a very dubious opening, but he found on inspection that his whiskers could just get through without touching either top or bottom. And, as where this is the case, the cat's body can always follow, he made it with a squeeze. And then Charley found himself on top of a porch with no means of getting back or getting down. This necessitated my opening the window widely and adjourning to the road outside armed with a handful of gravel to entice him to re-enter!

His first venture took him through a small space between the bathroom window and the wall of the house. Charley was discovered sunning himself on a window ledge fourteen

Younger cats may be more inclined to spend some time in the backyard playing or "hunting" than older ones, which prefer to stay indoors with all the niceties of home. Photo by Mrs. J. Judd.

A pair of bobcat kittens photographed in their natural habitat.

The bobcat or common American wildcat is found throughout the United States, eastern and western parts of Canada, and in Mexico. In nature, pumas pursue them. Notice the size differential between it and the Siamese cat. Photo by L. van der Meid.

Ocelots appear to be less fierce than other wild cats in the United States. However, it is not that easy to domesticate a jungle-born kitten. They are strong cats, about twice the size of a house cat, with formidable claws and teeth. Photo by L. van der Meid.

inches by five inches, with a fifteen foot drop below. Fortunately for Charley, the window opened inwards.

Cats vary a great deal in temperament. Our Mother Cat, a rather small grey and white, with a tiny face, needs love all the time. She adores beds, occupied or empty, and likes the occupier, if present, to extend a welcome at any time of the day or night, fondle her head and allow her to snuggle down on the counterpane.

Charley has no use for beds or their occupants. He is always on the defensive until he hears the food can being opened then he becomes surprisingly affectionate, rubbing his body around one's lower limbs until his saucer of food is resting on the ground. Then he is himself again. Charley is always on the *qui vive*, suspicious of every stranger and eager for the wide, open spaces—but a little nervous when they materialize.

There is a great likeness between cats and people.

III The Senses of the Cat

VISION

The cat has good nocturnal vision and it is often stated that a cat can "see" in the dark. This is a mistake since no animal can "see" unless there are at least *some* light rays available to stimulate the animal's retina and enable it to convey some visual impressions to the brain.

It is true that cats are able to hunt and even catch mice in conditions approaching darkness, but one has to take into account that the cat has a remarkable sense of hearing, and also the ability to record vibrations produced by movements of the prey.

Another possibility is that the cat, like the owl, may be able to recognize ultra-violet rays given off in darkness from the body of a mouse, or other animal.

It is true, however, that the cat is among the animals which see better than others after sunset—or in conditions approaching darkness—for various reasons.

Cats see in a dim light far better than we do because the cat possesses an iris, the pupil of which is able to dilate almost to the full diameter of the cornea—the transparent window of the eye.

In addition the cat's retina is well provided with rods for night use, even if the central cones are scanty. Night vision is bound up with chemical changes in these essential rods.

Incidentally, a cat can make use of its whiskers in darkness to find out how near it may be to other objects, and also

The reflective character of the eyes of cats is represented very well in this photograph of a leopard cat. This Asiatic wild cat is about the size of a domestic cat and is reported by some observers to be very fierce in the wild; other testimony indicates that the leopard cat can be tamed in captivity.

Opposite:
Observe the characteristic features and color pattern of this leopard cat, quite similar to those of an ordinary tabby cat.

whether or not there may be room between neighboring objects for his body to slide through. This is based on the supposition that when the whiskers can pass through without becoming bent, the whole cat can do likewise.

The iris of the cat, which is capable of dilating so fully, is also able to contract in a bright light to a mere upright slit, frequently with a pinhole-like aperture at either extremity of the slit. In a bright light, therefore, the cat can make use of what is equivalent to the old type of pinhole camera, which, in a good light, could feature on a flat plate objects near and far off, without focusing, and in either case obtain a clear image.

This does not imply that the cat lacks an otherwise normal focusing arrangement such as exists in many mammalian eyes (although it is not highly developed in the horse and in ruminants, which employ the "ramp retina").

A kitten with dilated pupils. Note that the iris is visible as an opaque ring in the periphery of the eye. The iris also bears the pigments that determine the color of the eyes. Photo by V. Baldwin.

The pupils of this cat are contracted and appear as narrow vertical slits. Emotional factors and the amount of light influence the condition of the cats' pupils as they do in other mammals. Photo by L. van der Meid.

But the cat makes little use of the structures designed to produce what is known as "accommodation" (altering the degree of convexity of the lens), and in bright daylight prefers to use its pupils on the principle of the pinhole camera, or of the more modern instamatic type of camera, which has a short focal length. In this way it obtains a clear picture at all distances without exercising any effort in the process.

But the pinhole mechanism, while very satisfactory between six and twenty feet in front of the cat's eyes, is not so good at very short range. Nocturnal vision is always short range, and for this the cat is compelled to employ the fully dilated pupil, and its retina, well supplied with rods.

Whether or not the cat is color blind has been a matter of controversy for many years. The general belief has always been that the cat, like the dog, saw all objects which to our eyes carried color in shades of grey. However, the more

A Scottish wild cat in repose. The wild cat in Great Britain was almost exterminated in the last century. It was considered as vermin and was purposely hunted down.

A close-up of the head of a Scottish wild cat. Note the slit-like pupils, tongue papillae, and canines. An incomplete set of front teeth indicates that it is fairly old.

modern theories suggest that the cat is a dichromat and a tritanonalous protanope. A dichromat is an individual able to match all colors with suitable mixtures of two, instead of the usual three primaries. A protanope also lacks something rather essential: he is red-blind.

The cat has particularly good vision with regard to moving objects but may miss a still one, such as a sitting mouse, until the moment that it moves. The cat then makes a spring towards the spot where it imagines the mouse will be. However, the mouse may change its mind, and freeze in its tracks. For a few moments the cat may be completely at a loss, since its focusing apparatus to near vision takes a little while to operate. By this time the mouse may have found cover close at hand.

If, however, the mouse decides to bolt in any direction, the eyes of the cat will recognize movement and the chances of escape on the part of the mouse will be very slight.

One may notice that when a cat plays with a mouse before killing it, the cat's paws come into constant use. This is an instance in which the sense of touch aids vision or may even replace it. The cat may appear at times unable to determine the whereabouts of the mouse when it is only a few feet in front of the cat's eyes.

Particularly in bright weather, when the cat's pupils are normally contracted, it will have quite good distance vision. A cat may immediately detect a sparrow sitting on the lawn twenty yards away (particularly if it moves), or a bird in the branches of a tree.

It will also note the presence of another cat fifty yards distant, especially if cat number two is violating the territorial rights of cat number one.

One cannot leave the subject of cat vision without reference to the "third eyelid" (*Membrana nictitans*), which is present in many of the quadrupeds, but absent in man. It is particularly well developed and often very apparent, in the Felidae.

The third eyelid of cats is seen in this photo as a dark membrane in the inner corners of each eye. Photo by S. Celeski.

The third eyelid works on the principle of the car windshield wiper. It protects the sensitive cornea against injury and removes any foreign matter which may alight on the surface of the eye.

At the back of the cat's eyeball is a pad of soft fat, which changes shape when it is compressed. The eyeball in the cat is provided with a retractor muscle which draws the eye back into the orbit, and causes it to squeeze the pad of fat. The third eyelid is attached to this pad and the movement in the fat draws the third eyelid rapidly upwards and over the eyeball. The prominence of the cat's eyes depends upon the amount of fat in the pads situated behind them. If a cat is in poor condition and lacking fat, the third eyelid may remain visible, partially covering the front of the eye. Owners are then apt to take their cat to the vet for eye treatment, when all it needs is de-worming and a few good meals!

A domestic cat enjoying one of the comforts of home, in this case a soft warm chair.

Opposite:
Appearance of a greatly frightened cat that is ready to fight. Note the unsheathed claws that are ready for action.

Siamese cat with the left ear deflected forward. Cats' ears, not as flexible as those of dogs, usually are kept upright. Photo by S. Celeski.

HEARING

The cat's ear structure is wonderfully well-developed.

The auditory sysem of the cat is dealt with in *Sensory Neurophysiology* by James C. Bondreau and Chiycko Tsuchitani, in 87 pages.

Basically, the cat becomes acquainted with all the normal sounds that occur within the home, particularly those relating to prospective meals. One of the writer's cats, "Charley," mentioned earlier in this book, can hear the movement of its saucer and the opening of a tin of food, when shut out in the garden fifteen feet from the partly-opened kitchen window.

Cats are nearly as clever as dogs in locating sounds and the direction from which sounds proceed, their only drawback being the rather rigid fixation of the ear cartilage, which necessitates turning the head and neck towards the required direction.

But the range of hearing in the cat is quite remarkable.

The writer's two cats previously described, Mother Cat and her son Charley, living in a country village with free run over wooded and pasture land, each have their separate hunting areas and seldom hunt together. These cats are trained to race back at mealtimes on signals mutually determined by the cats and their owner.

Routine cleaning of the ears is often uncalled for, except when excessive amounts of ear wax are noticed or the presence of ear mites is suspected. A Three Lions photo.

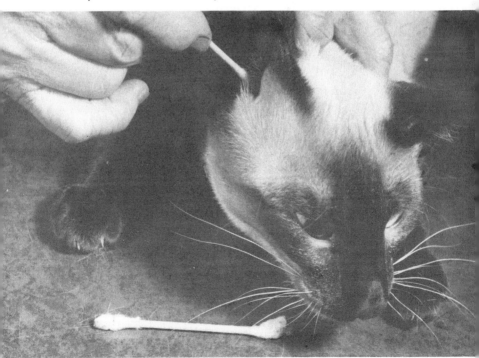

A long-haired breed of house cat, the Persian.

Opposite:
A typical short-haired cat, the Siamese.

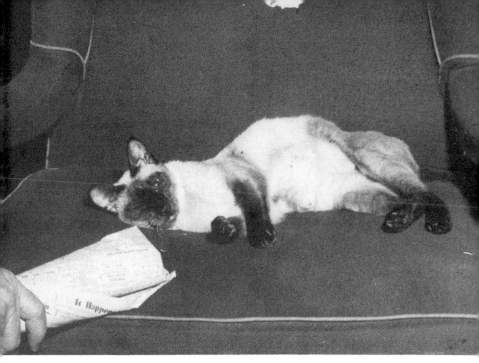

Short of physical force, it seems that this cat is bent on ignoring the owner's commands. It can hear well enough but is just too stubborn to pay any attention. A Three Lions photo.

When they are not far from home the signal is the tapping of a teaspoon on the inside of the kitchen window. Both cats hear this signal when approximately two hundred yards away (as the crow flies).

They hear the sound from a toy whistle when approximately a quarter of a mile away in two different directions and return home at full gallop.

Over shorter distances (up to one hundred yards) both cats respond to one of the supersonic (soundless) whistles employed for recalling dogs.

Cats do not, as a rule, associate themselves with the names given them by their owners, and do not usually come to call. This may be lack of understanding, or due to the cat's determination to obey no orders and to maintain complete independence.

I have recently completed a newspaper inquiry into the question of whether cats recognize other cats or dogs in television programs, and if so, how they react.

My own cats and dogs have all shown a complete indifference, even when the dogs and cats on the screen have displayed marked activity and produced a considerable amount of sound.

Readers of the newpaper contributed nearly a hundred accounts of interested responses by their own household pets. This indicates that out of many hundreds or thousands of homes which maintained both cats and a television set, at least one hundred animals showed some interest in the screen.

I have endeavoured to get a similar response from a considerable number of cats and dogs belonging to my friends and clients, without any success.

TASTE

The only indication one gets regarding the matter of taste as it concerns the cat is based on the cat's reaction to particular foods. All things that a cat will eat, even under duress, are not necessarily good for its health. The cat's urinary excretion has to be rigorously maintained otherwise the cat shows a marked tendency to develop urinary calculi, which, in the case of the castrated male with underdeveloped sex organs, may be critical.

Very few cats like water, especially when they can obtain milk, but they should be encouraged to drink clean fresh water, which should be always within reach.

Nowadays, when cats are fed mainly out of tins, one notices that some varieties of canned foods are refused while others are eaten gladly. This must be a question of taste and general palatability. Foods in firm chunks are not sought after unless they are crushed with a fork into a paste before offering them to the cat.

A litter of Siamese kittens. Note the almost identical markings and blue eyes that are characteristic of the breed.

Opposite:
Close-up of a variety of Siamese cat called seal point; dark parts are seal brown in color.

Most cats will eat commercially prepared cat food, but individual tastes vary greatly from one cat to another. Cats with very odd eating and drinking habits are not unheard of. Photo by L. van der Meid.

While some cats have a liking for fish and tins of food based on fish, other refuse it altogether, or eat insufficiently, to keep the cat in healthy condition.

Cats in the country catch and devour mice, voles, young rats and birds.

Very few cats will eat a shrew, although they may catch them in numbers. Occasionally, a young cat *will* eat a shrew, but for several (up to five) days afterwards it may refuse food of any kind.

Very few cats have any liking for sugar and sweet substances other than canned milk, which is often sweetened. In spite of this, quite a percentage of cats which refuse sugar will eat saccharine in their food.

A cat moved from its home to a boarding kennel will often refuse to eat altogether. Fasts of nine days have been recorded. Any household disturbance, even on occasion the arrival of new or strange furniture will on occasion turn the household cat off its food for up to forty-eight hours.

Hunting frogs for either food or fun is normal even for a domestic cat. Aquatic animals sustain many creatures in the wild, including small wild cats. Photo by H. Cate.

In the home there are various areas that are apparently preferred by most cats. Cats like to walk on top of fences, (above); sit on top of television sets, (opposite, upper photo), and stay under parked cars (opposite, lower photo)—which could be dangerous if the driver is unaware of their presence.

VARIOUS REFLEXES

Cats perform a number of typical reflex actions in response to stimuli. Those which have been tabulated include:

The Catnip Reflexes

This applies to contact with or attempts to eat *Napeta cataria*, the common catnip plant. This appears, even in neutered cats of either sex, to stimulate various manifestations of sexual activity. When close to it, cats will roll on the ground in apparent ecstasy. They will smell and lick the plant and occasionally nibble the tips of leaves.

A kitten eagerly jumping for a catnip ball. Even though this cat has not reached sexual maturity, the catnip response was spontaneous upon presentation of the ball. Photo by Francis G. Kern.

This black cat clutches the catnip ball with the front paws and digs reflexively at it with the hind legs. Photo by Kerry Donnelly.

Valerian has a similar influence on some cats, and in days long gone by, medical and veterinary students were apt to lay this substance on certain doorsteps, upon which all the stray cats of the neighborhood would congregate.

Cats appear to have a strong sense of smell and this undoubtedly influences their taste for certain foods. They smell fish wrapped in the family shopping, even before it can be unwrapped.

The Ear Reflex

Tickling the ear of a sleeping cat very gently with the tip of a feather induces violent flicking movements even if the cat continues to sleep. One need not actually apply the feather to the skin of the ear flap, any one of the long hairs protruding from inside the ear flap will produce the same reflex.

A stuffed teddy bear toy serves as a scratching post for this kitten. Scratching and stretching appear to be almost a daily activity in most cats.

The frayed condition of the upholstery of this chair is a mute testimony to the scratching tendencies of the cat.

In nature cats inevitably utilize trees as scratching surfaces. Big-game hunters are known to get their quarry by waiting for wild big cats at their favorite scratching spots.

The Proprioreceptor Factor

This is something which chiefly concerns cats, birds and tightrope walkers.

The proprioreceptor center is said to be situated somewhere in the body—nobody appears to know definitely just where—and it controls the sense of balance. It is supposed to tell you whether you are head up or head down when in midair. The cat is credited with the ability to fall from a rooftop, or a second-story window and to land always on its feet.

This is not entirely true, for many veterinary surgeons can mention cases in which the cat has landed head first, the most common injury being a cleft hard palate.

The ability to walk along a very narrow path is not a "trick" for a cat. The success an owner might have in making it repeat the action, however, is a different matter. A Three Lions photo.

Members of the cat family are known for their ability to spring for a large distance from a stationary position. House cats can and do jump for some things like catnip or a toy placed out of reach, as demonstrated here. A Three Lions photo.

It is true however that (as has been recorded in slow motion) the majority in falling from a height, will perform a regular series of motions while in midair, sometimes turning the body through 180° before rotating onto the back. It would appear that the changing of the body position in midair is a normal reflex action, but the timing may not be quite correct, depending largely upon the distance between the point of origin of the fall and the ground.

Note the great similarity between the attitudes of a big cat, a leopard (above) and a domestic cat (below) as they rest on trees.

An action shot of a domestic cat showing its agility and ability to jump across a natural barrier. Such feats are well known for feral animals but are less often practiced by house cats.

IV Communication

Like most domesticated animals, cats need to be able to communicate more or less with their owners and other human acquaintances, as well as be able to exchange ideas among their own kind. Dr. Kainz, an eminent psychologist, wrote in his book, *Animals Anthem,* the following words:

"So-called animal language never develops beyond certain rudimentary stages of human language. For man, these ways of communicating have not entirely lost their message but they are more important than his more characteristic methods. The concept of language is specifically human. It is to be applied to animals only if its meaning is considerably stretched and if far-fetched metaphors are allowed in describing its content."

The cat has a rather more limited or less demonstrative vocabulary than the dog has with very few exceptions, and makes far less use of its voice. Fortunately, however, cats do not bark. Nevertheless, the cat has one advantage over the dog in being able to advertise a positive state of mind by purring, and in association with its human companions it makes great use of this ability.

There has been much discussion among scientists as to the mechanism of purring. It is thought to originate in the larynx of the cat and appears to be produced by rapid vibration—a tremolo—of the vocal cords. Although several observers prefer the theory that by some nervous control, or otherwise, blood is forced through the vessels of the larynx at an extraordinary rate. Seeing that the tone can be varied at

Cats utter different types of sounds, but contact is the most direct means of communication among them. Photo by K. Donnelly.

will by the cat, ranging from a low mellow sound to a considerably higher pitch, the odds would appear to be very much in favor of a voluntary muscular vibration of the vocal cords. This is particularly noticeable in the Manx cat and to some extent in the Siamese, though the latter breed is more given to definite articulation than a sound as modest as a purr.

Purring is usually regarded as a sign of contentment and appeasement, of affection for its owner, and acceptance of a stranger. None the less, a cat will purr for its own enjoyment even while entirely alone. But it has also been noted, in boarding kennels in which feline influenza is a dreaded disease, that cats that purr too frequently or all through the day are often victims of the disease in its incubative stage.

In order to survive wild cats catch prey by stealth or stalking (lying low and walking cautiously towards the objective). Domestic cats instinctively stalk too in spite of the absence of the need to get their own food. Shown facing and above are domestic cats in stalking positions.

By the stance she's taken and the sounds she's made, this spitting mother cat has no difficulty letting anyone know that she means business and is ready to deal with intruders. A Three Lions photo.

Spitting is another sound that enters into the cats vocabulary range. It in no way refers to the human action described by the word and usually signifies the opposite state of mind as purring. A cat spits when it has been put on the defensive or feels its own well being, or that of its young in the case of a mother cat, is in danger, or when it is aggressively engaged in doing battle with another cat. It also emits this rather indescribable sound to ward off interlopers who have trespassed in its territory. Spitting frequently accompanies other methods of communications, such as an arched back or raised fur when the cat has been made to feel fearful or intends to attack.

It does not require much to realize whether cats are fighting or playing. Each of these activities is accompanied by sounds that can easily be identified. Photo by K. Donnelly.

It must be remembered too that the cat has an ability to detect sounds very much higher in pitch than our own ears are capable of hearing. The ears of the cat can pick out the minute noises made by infant mice in the nest. These are very high-pitched squeaks which human ears cannot appreciate. Cats are able to determine sounds on frequency levels up to 60 kcs., while the unaided human ear can hear nothing over 20 kcs. It is possible, therefore, that the domestic cat can emit sounds far higher in pitch than anything we are able to detect, yet which are perfectly audible to other cats. The cat also hears and often responds to the high-pitched whistle, inaudible to human ears, commonly used in handling sheepdogs.

Different kinds of cats possess different voices and among the oriental breeds, the Siamese probably comes out on top as possessor of the greatest variety of voice sounds. As I have mentioned in my book, *How Animals Talk,* my closest friend

In the home area cats usually walk with independence and non-chalance; they are aware of the absence of predators within the con-fines of the house and its surroundings. The cat shown above and the two shown opposite, for example, are relatively unconcerned about the presence of potential dangers—they're looking for adven-ture.

It is not too difficult to imagine that a characteristic type of sound accompanies the attitude of these kittens. Note the bared teeth and unsheathed claws, possibly a reaction to being cornered against a wall with no means of escape.

during my early teens was a female Siamese cat that had been given to me because nobody else could endure her presence. Her very inappropriate name, Wun Lung, provided no indication of her vocal ability! She possessed the loudest and most enviable voice that any living animal could have possessed, and she appeared able to carry on a continuous conversation during the whole day and a considerable portion of the night, in persistent but variable tones. What's worse was that none of the sounds that emerged from that charming little mouth appeared to have any meaning whatever.

Wun Lung also seemed to have no comprehension of the meaning of human speech or its purpose. She was equally unimpressed by words of endearment, commands, or heated abuse. She kept up the same persistent monologue if she was being presented with a saucerful of salmon, or being chased out into the garden.

Her one clear and evident intention was never to get far out of the sight and hearing distance of her young owner, and in spite of everything I did to escape her attention, Wun Lung had, by some miraculous power, the ability to seek me out and attach herself to my person wherever I might hap-

Cats can spend much time intertwined with one another, possibly for warmth and companionship.

Cats enjoy water not only for drinking, like this cat is lapping water with its tongue, but also to get into occasionally. However, they could get ill drinking heavily chlorinated water from swimming pools.

Right and below:
Flat dishes are better than deep bowls for feeding cats, especially if several cat are to share the meal. Whether or not cats will share food depends on the temperature and training of the cat. Adults are often more reluctant to share their food than are kittens who have been brought up with this practice.

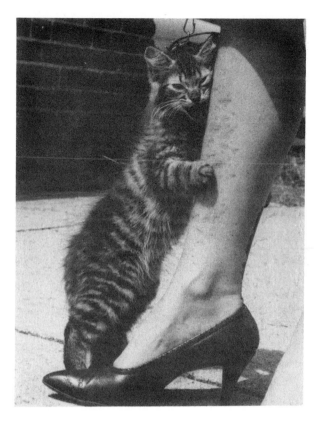

The hazards of owning a cat include hosiery runs for ladies and frayed trousers for men. Inevitably, a cat finds that brushing on its owner's legs is the best way of delivering a message or getting attention. A Three Lions photo.

pen to be. And quite often this occurred at some distance from home.

The greatest trouble arose when she discovered the school at which I was studying for my entrance exams to the Royal Veterinary College. She would arrive apparently from nowhere in the middle of a lesson and from then on hold the stage with her voice as much as with her beauty.

The climax came when I had to attend a meeting of solicitors after I had been called to give evidence in a speeding offense. Hardly had the proceedings begun when Wun Lung suddenly appeared, jumped onto the bench beside me and broke into her persistent monologue. With arched back and unsheathed claws, she dared any of the officials to remove her from the room.

Much against my will at this time of my life, I was compelled to give up churchgoing in case Wun Lung decided to follow me and take part in the service.

Cats as a rule, are not given to open conversation among themselves, except when courting or out on the warpath. My own two black and white cats, mother and son, intertwine in one armchair in such a way that anyone who did not know them might imagine they were seeing some strange-colored animal, possessed of one head and five legs. They would also observe that never a sound comes from this strange creature until the two cats are wakened and realize that food is not far away.

The tail is a good indicator of a cat's disposition. After enough time observing a particular cat, one can tell whether it is happy, angry, or unconcerned. Photo by L. van der Meid.

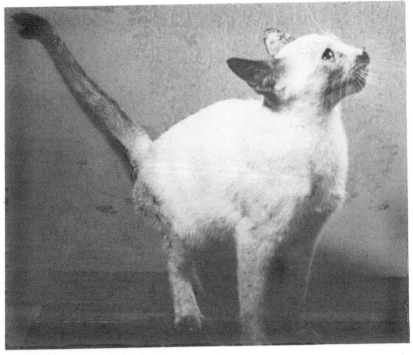

Mama cat and its young. Note the great variability of the color pattern of this litter. Just like any other member of the cat family, the mother carries the young by the neck, (below).

A most endearing pose of two sleeping friends, a puppy and a kitten. In the wild fear of predators is instilled by the mother cat before the kittens leave the mother's care to fend for themselves.

Cats make their own particular sounds in connection with definite purposes. For example, the plaintive mew uttered by the cats sitting at the kitchen door asking to be let out into the garden, is entirely different from the louder, more raucous sound the same cat makes when it is usually, in its own opinion, on the wrong side of a door. Then again, most cats when entering a room make use of a soft musical note which one might almost translate into "Hello!"

The sense of smell plays a prominent part in communication between animals and probably between animals and man, since the bodies of white people give off an odor not recognized by other whites but quite apparent to cats, as well as to black people. The intensity of the human body odor varies according to the degree to which the person concerned is friendly towards the cat or other animals present, including members of the human race. When one is annoyed or merely bored, the cat's very perceptive sense of smell can determine the state of its owner's temper as much by the smell emanating from him or her as from the tone of voice.

The cat's tail is another means of communitcation it makes use of. But the wagging of a cat's tail is quite different in its meaning from the wagging of a dog's tail. When the cat carries its tail curved over an arched back with fur standing on end, it is using its tail to express marked displeasure.

Many cats have their own special means of wheedling their human companions into taking notice, a preliminary to asking for food. Rubbing their bodies against one's legs is a common method. Another is to jump onto a chair or table to attract attention with a similar objective in view. If all else fails, a wise cat will usually situate itself on a chair or low table, midway in between the owner's chair and the T.V. screen.

V Habits Feline

My dictionary defines a habit as an automatic response to specific situations, acquired normally as a result of repetition and learning, strictly applicable only to motor responses. I must disagree with this definition in some ways as it applies to the cat.

Let us take for example, the habit of cleaning, or grooming, a procedure almost identical in every way in every member of the species and yet highly technical. The procedure in a three-months-old kitten is identical to that of its mother who may be three years old. Although cat mothers clean their babies almost from the moment of birth until they are at weaning point, the maternal effort will come to a sudden stop then and the kitten will be perfectly qualified to carry out the process for itself in every detail. Nobody has ever seen, so far as I can ascertain, any mother cat giving an infant any instruction in how to carry out this process.

By the sixth week every kitten should be grooming itself in precisely the way and order with which mother cat grooms itself. From its third month and throughout the remainder of its life, the cat will groom itself on the slightest provocation, such as after being stroked or petted, after meals, after defecation, following actual contact with another cat or any other animal. It will also repeat the process if bored and if children's advances are made towards it accompanied by stroking or cuddling. I have heard it remarked on many occasions, that the family cat makes use of anything as an excuse for a good scrub-up!

Various poses of kittens learning how to use the fore-paws: Defensive attitude against possible frontal threat (above); pouncing on small animals, possibly like some insects (opposite, upper photo); and holding on an object, like a piece of ribbon (opposite, lower photo).

Self-grooming is one of the many activities of cats. Paws are first wet with saliva and then rigorously licked. Photo by K. Donnelly.

During the cleaning activity, the face receives the earliest attention. The cat will dampen the inside of its forelimb below the knee with saliva, then wipe the eyes, the cheeks, and around and behind the ears, as well as its chin. The cat adopts a number of characteristic poses, common to all cats, while cleaning all parts of the body. One leg at a time is held upright in the air, followed by the others in regular turn.

By the time the cat has completed the toilet, it will have wiped or licked every inch of the body, apart perhaps from a line down the middle of the spine, which may be a little difficult if the cat happens to be very fat or pregnant. Occasionally two cats that happen to be friends will groom one another.

As kittens nurse, a mother cat grooms her young affectionately at the same time. Photo by L. van der Meid.

Grooming is a common pursuit of friendly cats. Photo by K. Donnelly.

Cats and dogs tolerate each other, especially if a kitten is born in the same household as the dog.

Opposite:
Young cats like to stay close to their mother, so close that it may be difficult to determine where one body begins and the other ends, as in this photo.

PLAYING

In the kitten, play from an early age is not only amusing but it is also educational. As soon as they have acquired the ability to walk, or at least to control body movements, kittens will instinctively pursue, pounce upon, claw at and make attempts to bite at any small object which moves. The bodily movements will be accompanied by posturing and swaying the body before pouncing. This is a pattern of behavior which is not learned or acquired, but is purely instinctive

A kitten in a quandary as to what to do with a duckling. The instinct to pursue a moving object will eventually come to the kitten. Photo by L. van der Meid.

A cat can treat almost anything, even a loosely hanging string, as a toy. Photo by K. Donnelly.

and a genetic legacy. It is a feature common to all cats quite independent of learning, and does not appear to have any particular use. The use of hunting, on the other hand, which its play often mimics, is a necessity if the kitten is to live from weaning age to adult growth. But this knowledge is acquired step by step and its acquisition needs a deal of time. Hunting something not good to eat is purely a waste of time and the kitten learns not only what is fit to eat, but also to avoid hunting which is purely time wasted. The development of appetite and the wish and ability to eat are instinctual tendencies in most young animals which compel him to learn to hunt.

Just like humans, cats may habitually occupy certain spots within the home, such as a window sill, under a chair, or atop a table as shown on this page and opposite. They may resist leaving their spot or "territory."

In comparison to dogs there is less activity during nursing time in cats. Apparently each kitten is "assigned" to a nipple, so normally no struggle for getting the best position is needed. Photo by L. van der Meid.

Before the kitten is weaned and almost from the day of birth, a system of teat ownership develops in the nest, whereby each kitten lays claim to a teat that is to be shared by no other, unless by mistake when a neighbor is otherwise occupied. The result is that a whole litter can be actively engaged, all at the same time, in suckling without fuss or opposition. This is opposed to behavior in young puppies in which the strongest grabs the best teat high up in the groin and defends it against all comers. While the next strongest puppy moves one teat forward, the pattern is repeated until the weakest puppy is attached to one of the front teats which provides the least milk.

Proper coordination and balance are the results of what seems to appear as just the playing and clowning of very young kittens. By repetition they learn to walk, climb, jump, etc. A Three Lions photo.

Almost anything can be amusing to a cat. A Christmas tree ball is not safe from the clutches of a cat. However, when such decorations accidentally break, it can cut the lips and paws.

A bouncing ball can offer much entertainment and exercise to both young and adult cats.

Swatting or probing with the paws is a form of play that is generally an extension of a cat's predatory instincts.

Any free-rolling object, like a ball or a spool provided as toys to kittens, can improve eye coordination and leg movements. Photo by V. Baldwin.

In winter, the kittens lie close to one another to conserve heat, but in warm summer weather the bodies are straggled all over the nest to provide ventilation. Young kittens, as soon as they acquire use of their legs, will play games with one another in which one takes the part of the hunter and the other the prey. The positions may be reversed from time to time. It is obvious from the nature of the play that there is no intention to wound or injure the kitten taking the part of the prey. That comes later when living mice, or birds, and mice still conscious, are brought to the nest by the mother. One might also say that the activities during this form of play are somewhat exaggerated and display a little more showmanship than would be necessary if one were out to kill and devour. Play is obviously meant to provide enjoyment as well as education. It promotes physical fitness and, in a way, somewhat resembles the activities of a youth using a punchball! It stimulates a knowledge of footwork, rapid movement, and keeps young kittens in or around the nest during their mother's absence on a more serious hunting expedition.

Play in the kitten does not stop as it grows, but can be induced in most adult cats if one provides an artificial "prey." A cotton reel rolled along the ground, or a pingpong ball threaded on a cord make admirable toys, while a clockwork mouse may provide great excitement—while the mouse lasts. As soon as it begins to disintegrate it must be discarded to prevent small parts from being swallowed.

Adult cats are also fascinated by mobile toys. The motions are akin to those utilized by wild cats in catching prey. Photo by L. van der Meid.

Extremes in the color of the fur are desired by cat fanciers, with all-white cats on one end of the spectrum and completely black cats on the other end.

Two cats at play. The upper black and white cat is in the act of nipping at the neck of the black cat. Photo by K. Donnelly.

Older cats, especially those in good homes, will play together when the mood takes them in very much the same way as kittens. The main difference is that adults regard one another in a different way. The cat being hunted becomes a rabbit instead of a mouse, and the tactics adopted would apply to hunting the larger animal rather than to that of the smaller. Both cats may even jump over each other's body in the process.

A great deal of the play indulged in, both by kittens and by grown cats, is directed towards learning how to attack, how to time the attack, and how to balance the body on the ground and in midair. The play of young animals in some ways resembles the behavior of a young person learning to shoot a gun. It involves learning how to aim correctly, the

Two-day-old kittens. Suckling is the main activity for the next ten days. The eyes open a few days later. Photo by D. Martin.

feline counterpart being to learn when to put action into execution. The youth must learn the exact moment to pull the trigger, while the cat must learn the precise moment to fly through the air for the attack. All of this practice is absolutely essential if the cat is one that will have to hunt for its living rather than be fed a saucer of prepared food four times a day.

Every kitten, from the time of birth, follows a regular program observed by the young of all irrespective of breed or environment. On the third day of its life the kitten acquires the use of one particular nipple from its mother's breast and literally hangs on to it during the whole of its suckling period. By the 11th or 12th day the eyes will be open, and by the 21st day most of the kittens in the litter will be able to stand and move around in the nest. By the 28th day, they will have commenced to climb around walls or ledges pertaining to the nesting place and may even travel short distances from the nest and back again.

In the wild state kittens begin to leave the nest and follow their mother for short distances, then leave her and return to the nest. By the time they are six weeks old they will have commenced to play with any small, movable objects in the nest or its vicinity. By the eighth week, the kittens may have arguments among themselves, starting with play and ending up in actual aggression. Most of the play among kittens is directed towards learning to recognize objects simulating small animals, at short range, and devising methods of capturing them.

Playing and "fighting" go together. Note the kitten in the background being batted on the snout. Photo by L. van der Meid.

Handling with the forepaws of some small rounded object by an eight-week kitten is equivalent to handling a mouse, and is a simple modification of normal adult behavior. Cats are dependent upon the sharpness of their claws, either for catching small game on the ground or for jumping into the air and bringing down birds taking flight. For this purpose, they sharpen their nails daily on a log of wood, or upon the leg of a dining room table, whichever may be immediately available.

Typical pose of a kitten learning how to handle a slippery object, in this instance a rubber ball. Photo by V. Baldwin.

Many pet owners provide their pets with scratching posts in order to save the furniture from claw marks. Photo by K. Donnelly.

FIGHTING

This is indulged in as a matter of principle by adult "toms." Cats under eighteen months old rarely fight though they may go through some of the antics, mainly in the guise of play. But fights between cats are always a serious matter and the submission gesture common among other animals, does not appear to have been adopted. The loser makes his escape if possible, but he may be chased by the winner and again brought down. Fights to the death are by no means rare.

It might be mentioned here that veterinary surgeons are frequently called upon to deal with the 'tail-less cat.' This is the cat that arrives home in the morning with only the stump of a tail, usually in country areas but not always, in these times. The supposition is that the cat has been attacked by a cattle dog or has been caught by the tail in a rabbit gin. In a few cases, when the culprit has been traced, it was found that neither the cattle dog nor the trap was to blame. The guilty party was a big dog fox who could run just fast enough to catch the cat's tail—but not the entire cat!

SLEEPING

It has been estimated that the ordinary house cat which is regularly fed and has no hunting to do, spends three-quarters of its life asleep. Nor is it very particular about where it sleeps or under what conditions.

This picture illustrates the complete disregard of where and with whom a cat will sleep. Photo by L. van der Meid.

A rolled-up sleeping position that is reminiscent of many animals
sleeping in the wild. Photo by K. Donnelly.

Charley, the writer's neutered male, seems to prefer sleeping in the open air and will balance himself on top of a four-
inch wooden garden gate, seven feet off the ground, exposed
to wind and weather. He will sleep in this position for as
long as two hours at a time, oblivious to the traffic passing
six feet away. His mother, however, has her own favorite
armchair and sleeps either in this or on a mat in front of the
fire.

As an alternative, either or both will curl up on the hood of
the car, kept in a drive alongside the house. The hood is
covered with mackintosh material and is frequently slightly
warm after the car returns from a run through the town.
Quite often the two will curl into a solid ball in the armchair

in a variety of positions, and it would be difficult at first glance to decide which portion of a body belonged to which cat, seeing that they are both marked out in black and white. Such sleeps are very sound and when their chair is required for some other purpose, it is possible to lift out the two cats on the cushion which contains them and deposit them, still asleep, onto another chair.

Cats appear able to sleep, or to go into a trance, when seated on a rug in front of a fire and apparently gazing into the flames. They will sit in this position without moving for as much as an hour at a time. They are not, as dogs are, the

Two common sleeping positions of cats.

The fondness of cats for beds can not be over-emphasized, particularly if there are warm bodies already in it. Photo by L. van der Meid.

least bit particular about where or how they sleep, but appear to be able to lie in any apparently uncomfortable box, or other situation, turn off a switch, and immediately drop off into a sound sleep that may last for an hour, or a whole night. They are, however, particularly fond of beds, preferably unmade and still containing what the cat regards as the odor of the preceding occupant. To crawl into bed alongside an unprotesting child is a delight indeed and one should be very particular about leaving a baby asleep wherever there is a cat which might ensconce itself on top of the baby. Many fatalities, primarily from suffocation, have occurred in this way throughout the years.

Cats appear to fall into one of two kinds of sleep. In the sleep more common throughout the day, the muscles do not completely relax but maintain a state of mild tonus. Blood pressure is reduced but the body temperature rises 1 to 2 degrees Fahrenheit. In the deep sleep, the muscles relax, blood pressure is markedly lowered and the body temperature tends to fall, more or less, according to the situation and the presence of drafts. In both the light and the deep sleep the cat's auditory reflexes remain very alert. A cat will become completely awake and ready to make its escape at any unexpected noise. Noises customary in any situation, such as a machine at work, a whistle or a hooter, may cause no reaction, but dropping a stone or a piece of wood—an unexpected sound—will produce immediate response and suitable reactions.

Apparently cats dream, in the sense that they "see" certain happenings and may react as though they were awake. In this matter cats are not exceptional, as a dog may "gallop" while still asleep and give rise to vocal efforts suggesting that it is in "full cry!"

VI Feline Intelligence

One may wonder what goes on within the mind of the cat and whether it has any inherent or acquired ability to think or reason. The two are not entirely the same. Thinking implies a definite course of ideas. In the stricter sense, it implies a course of ideas initiated by a problem. During this flow of ideas, one of the ideas may appear to possess exceptional advantages, and on these grounds it may meet with acceptance, others being at least temporarily discarded. An idea may also be discarded because past experience has shown it to be dangerous, or to possess other disadvantages. Thoughts develop after—and out of—experience. Reasoning may be associated with the search for security or for comfort or pleasure. It also provides an essential safeguard against possible dangers.

Modern psychologists still refuse to accept the belief that animals of lesser intelligence than man are able to summon up mental figures, otherwise known as ideas, compare their values and finally select one or more best adapted to the problem under consideration. They claim that these animals are unable to reason. They appear to overlook the fact that the cat, one of the so-called lower animals, may be completely able to maintain itself, without help, from the time it is six months old, while a human child from the most enlightened stock, is unable to walk for many months following its birth has to be taught to wash and keep itself clean, is completely incompetent for the first four years of its life, and is not

Regardless of consequences, cats will attempt to occupy the softest and most comfortable spots in the house. A Three Lions photo.

regarded as being able to live a separate existence away from its parents until it is eighteen years of age.

If a cat takes a casual walk on a wintry day and ends it by sitting on a pile of stones, it may summon up a mental picture of a warm room containing a warm sofa and a coal fire. If it is able to visualize the two situations and decide which it would prefer, and can then translate its idea into bodily movement, surely this is very akin to thinking. The psychologists would prefer to believe that every separate activity of this particular cat arises from a response to some particular stimulus. The cat is not an automaton and its activities are not inspired entirely by instinct alone, but also by suitable response to mental stimuli of its own development.

The cat is one of the few animals capable of being domesticated which is still able to live in a wild state without human help, although it will condescend to share its life with human beings and enjoy so doing. Even then, the cat retains its independence and if not treated with respect, well fed, and given the best armchair, it feels quite at liberty to walk back into the wild and decide later on whether or not it will give domestication a further trial. Much may depend upon the weather at the time!

One of every cat's steadfast principles is a refusal to obey orders of any kind and to decide for itself the course of action it will take on any particular occasion. One can speak to a dog when it tends to beg at table. One commands "Bed" or "Chair," or "Out!" and the dog instantly obeys. To say any

A cat bent on not being led. With the hind legs firmly implanted on the pavement it is not about to follow the pull forward. With one flick of the head it can possibly slip through a fairly large collar. A Three Lions photo.

A good harness and leash for a Siamese or any other cat. The possibility of strangling or choking the animal is greatly reduced; traction is applied on the chest instead of the neck. Photo by L. van der Meid.

of these to the cat would be mere waste of time. Your dog will permit you to place a collar around its neck, slip on a lead, and walk it for a quarter of an hour along a road which holds no interest for it whatever. It is obeying orders. A few kittens, mainly Siamese, have been taught to wear a collar and lead, but once on the lead the cat takes *you* for a walk. It is the cat who decides where it will go.

None of the foregoing implies that your cat is not prepared to display affection when in the mood to be fussed over and petted. It is willing to cooperate on equal terms, for just as long as it pleases. You will be permitted to stroke its head, tickle its neck and ears and scratch the back of its neck.

Frequently the cat will sit on your knees, paddle with its front feet, and make funny little sounds with its mouth and lips which may be very impressive until you discover that your clothing which the cat has been sucking is now wet through with saliva, and that the cat's nails have lifted the stitches out of your outer garments. This operation is known as "singing its thrums." Nobody quite knows the meaning or intention behind this feline exercise, but is usually originates from a female cat and is supposed to illustrate the emotional atmosphere inseparable from a recent maternity.

The cat is completely devoid of any moral sense in its dealing with members of the household. Charley, the writer's cat, rescued with its mother from a nest in the wilds, adopted and brought up in the midst of great respectability, will very gently open a cupboard door, creep inside, close the door and entirely consume the slice of steak left therein. Then he will leave the cupboard, close the door behind him, and retire to enjoy a nice sleep on the mat in front of the drawing room fire. Confronted later with the empty plate, he will adopt an air of innocence, be completely at a loss to recognize the plate or even why I bother to show it to him. No missionary among the heathens could be wasting his time more completely than I have done.

The cat is not a highly trainable animal but not because it lacks intelligence. It is by nature entirely uncooperative. In many ways it is a highly inquisitive animal, but its curiosity elicited by unrecognized objects is not concerned with the desire to acquire knowledge, but only with whether the material may be something good to eat. Psychologists haven't gotten too far with cats in intelligence tests, mainly because no self-respecting cat will allow itself to be exploited in this manner. Cats have a marked dislike for repeating some set operation a number of times just to provide evidence of intellectual capability. Nor can a cat be bribed. A saucer of milk or food may be quite acceptable in the usual way, but if one thinks that any sensible animal is going to sit

Cats can purr when petted or other times when they appear content. Photo by L. van der Meid.

up and beg, jump through hoops, or dance on its hind legs, all for a bit of food or sausage, one had better try it on a dog.

In return for love and kindness most cats, particularly females, will purr softly and delicately. Purring in the cat has been the subject of a deal of controversy, but, as mentioned previously, probably depends upon an ability to

Any abandoned building can serve as a den where stray cats can raise a family until they are "evicted" by health inspectors.

vibrate the vocal cords within the larynx, and it has been associated by some scientists with an increased flow of blood through the blood vessels within the laryngeal region. The intensity of the purring sound may vary greatly in intensity in accordance with the nature of the stimulus giving rise to the reflex activity. A gentle continuous purring may coincide with the feeding of kittens, increasing to a crescendo under conditions approaching a feline ecstasy, and undoubtedly setting into operation in such cases a definite vibration of the vocal cords.

THE ANGRY CAT

Cats are not always to be found in an angelic mood. Most of their tantrums are associated either with territorial disputes or amorous competition. Anger is at once signified in the cat's face. Almost immediately the body stiffens, the coat stands up on end, the legs straighten and the back arches. The pupils of the eyes in the angry cat immediately contract to small slits and the ears lie back flat against the sides of the head. The tail is one of the first parts of the body to give the danger signal. It becomes erect and in a long-coated cat it fluffs out to its full width. Under such conditions the cat loses all fear and will face a dog three times its size, or a bull, with equal ferocity. Any cat in this state is not a creature with which one should take risks. Its amazing activity enables it to change its ground very frequently and to make changes in position far more rapidly than the enemy can deal with.

One aged tabby cat, a female, owned by the writer when he was a boy, would lie behind the yard gate leading into the main village street, in wait for its arch enemy, a large terrier dog, which would then be on its way home. As soon as the dog came within reach, the cat would dive around the door, leap onto the dog's back, fix its position with teeth and claws and remain in this position while the dog, screaming, bolted for home. This happened on several occasions, until the dog found another route.

VII Territorial Behavior

It is generally accepted that most wild animals cherish the belief that at least certain parts of the kingdom they inhabit are their own private property and that no other animal, large or small, has the right to enter it. This so-called territorial habit is not so highly marked in cats as it is in the dog family, probably because cats are somewhat nomadic in nature, tend to move quickly from place to place, and are not large or strong enough to be the aggressors, ever ready to fight to the death.

In fact many cats, at least members of the domesticated variety, are discarded by their owners and pushed out to starve, as is the case with so many kittens after the Christmas festivities. Parents decide between themselves that the kitten given to the children by Aunt Sarah on Christmas day is not exactly what the children need, and the Father should drop it into an empty garden on his way back to work after the holiday is over. Such a start in life is not quite the best incentive to establishing a territory of one's own and this applies to a high percentage of homeless cats.

Puppies, unwanted and thrown onto a rubbish heap, usually die of starvation unless someone finds them and gives them food until they "find it a good home." Even then, a large number return to their dust heaps as soon as the novelty of owning a puppy wears off. Cats are more capable than dogs, of looking after themselves, catching and killing prey for food, and moving to fresh sites when the first one

It is unfortunate whenever gift pets are not appreciated or protected and are abandoned to fend for themselves outside the home. Photo by B. Taylor.

draws a blank. On this account the territorial instinct never becomes very active.

In certain areas, however, cats without homes congregate. A well-known site is the old Coliseum in Rome which is now the home of scores of homeless cats that make use of the protection it affords. In this warm climate the cats form groups and breed and multiply in numbers. It appears that certain good-natured people provide some food for their favorites, but on the whole the tendency is for these "feral" cats, as cats which have "gone wild" are termed, to stay shy of humanity and live only for food and sex. Such an existence could only be tolerable in a warm country.

It must not be forgotten that such large colonies of unvaccinated cats from a great many parts of the country are a potential hotbed of infestation both of infective diseases and contagious skin diseases. In addition, nearly all are infested with bowel parasites and deposit the eggs and larvae in the parts of the city they inhabit. Such larvae can infect children, who may develop meningitis and possibly suffer serious consequences. Cats, looked after in a kind home and taken to the veterinary surgeon to be vaccinated and freed from bowel parasites, can be charming pets for children but if they are neglected they can become a family danger.

To abandon a house cat during the winter is particularly cruel. The cold and scarcity of food can quickly kill a discarded pet cat. Photo by S. Thompson.

Not every country has its Coliseum, but nearly every country village has some old ruin, or some "animal lovers" who provide food for stray cats. And many an empty house or cottage has its four-legged squatters. Lost cats have a knack for getting together and living free apart from the demands of humanity. On the other hand, a kitten taken from the nest as soon as it is safely weaned, will settle down in the home of any family who will feed and look after it in the style it considers adequate. Usually it will make no organized attempt to leave this home for another, even if the opportunity arises. Such a kitten is more likely to develop territorial instincts and regard the garden and precincts of the house as "home," rather than one that does not share an abode with human beings and relies solely on its own resources for self-survival.

Fortunately, most pet cats are neutered by the time they are six months old. If this were neglected, a male kitten would walk around "spraying" the boundaries of its territory at quite frequent intervals and the smell of the urine of an "undoctored" male cat is sufficiently potent to raise doubts in the mind of the owners as to the virtues of the territorial instinct. The female kitten on the other hand will, as soon as it has achieved puberty, take frequent little walks from home, anointing the paths in each direction with little drops of urine which by our standards would be regarded as odorless.

But to the feline Casanova, each of these droplets conveys a number of meanings. Firstly, the position of the house where the lady cat lives, is made quite clear from whichever direction it may be approached. Then there is another message. Each consecutive deposit on the pavement indicates the exact stage of the donor's oestrous cycle and provides a very good indication of the particular day of the week on which one would be invited to "come up and see me sometimes!" The end result is that on one particular day, out of a possible few months, there will be an immense cater-

A stranded cat in a tree is a common problem in many urban areas. The chore of bringing down such cats is the responsibility in many cases of the fire department, the police, or the rescue squad of towns and cities.

Climbing trees is not too hard to learn. Coming down, however, is a different story. A Three Lions photo.

wauling in your village, and all the male cats in the vicinity will be ensconsed in your garden. The antidote to all this, of course, is to take your female kitten to the veterinary surgeon when it is five months old and have it spayed.

Cats, particularly those of the feral type, often include high trees, such as ash, elm and poplar, in their territorial domain. The frequency with which local fire brigades are called out to rescue cats from high trees is quite remarkable, but cats appear to have no fear of heights and often get into the top branches of an elm or poplar and can find nothing to drop back to which will support their weight. As a result they stay, sometimes for days, in the uppermost branches in which they cannot be seen. Neither do their plaintive cries reach ground level.

The object of tree-climbing is not only the hope of catching birds but the more tangible prospect of finding a nest containing young birds. The result is that this happens almost invariably during spring and summer, when the trees are in full foliage, which creates a good cover, hiding tree-climbing cats from view. There is, however, one set of circumstances which may lead one to suspect that a cat is present in the tree and this is provided by all the local jackdaws and starlings that gather to mob the cat, no longer able to protect itself and concerned with doing all it can to maintain

Besides trees, cats also like to sit and sun themselves atop stone walls. Photo by McCrea.

For this cat an antique oven serves as a private parking place. Photo by L. van der Meid.

a safe position. The birds have their own peculiar cries used in mobbing operations, which are entirely dissimilar to those used on ordinary occasions.

Some cats have a fascination for chimneys. Our own neutered Charley has his own cubbyhole in the wall of the kitchen, entered by diving through an aperture in a dresser which lacks a drawer. When a stranger, especially a man such as the one who reads the electric meter, makes a sudden appearance, Charley normally dives for the kitchen wall.

But, when circumstances stand in his way, he will shoot up the nearest available chimney, one attached to an unlighted grate, and will stay out of sight until the intruder has gone.

One of my lady clients owned a black cat and on one occasion, when she brought it to my waiting room, she took it out of the basket and sat it on her knee until the advent of a man with an Alsatian dog, upon his entry the cat bolted up the chimney. It made a reappearance five days later when someone observed the head of a black cat looking out over one of the chimney pots on the surgery roof. The services of the local fire brigade were needed to effect its complete removal. Fortunately, as my client remarked, the experience appeared to have cured the cat of whatever it was she had brought the cat for in the first place.

A carrying case can greatly reduce the opportunity to escape during a visit to the veterinarian or anywhere else. Of course, your cat will find confinement objectionable. Photo by L. van der Meid.

We experienced another remarkable case of the disappearing cat in that same waiting room. A lady brought a tortoiseshell female cat to the waiting room, took it out of the basket and settled it down on a neighboring chair. After this she entered into close conversation with another client in the room and when her turn came to enter the consulting room, there was no cat. The windows and doors had been closed and there appeared to have been no means of escape—but the cat had vanished. Further examination though revealed the fact that the lady had sat with her back to a cupboard, the door of which may have been slightly ajar. When the interior of this cupboard was inspected it was found that there was a loose board, one which could be moved to one side, leaving a small opening into the wall, although at the time the board was in position. Nine days later we heard a mewing coming from behind the skirting board running along the floor of one of the consulting rooms some distance from the waiting room and on a slightly higher level. When the skirting board was removed the cat, extremely dusty but apparently unharmed, walked out.

It appeared when the cavity was swept out, that a number of the polished wing cases of beetles and blackbeetles were to be found in the sweepings and it is possible that the cat had eaten the bodies. There had been no opportunity for drink and yet the cat appeared well, though a little thin. This tallies with the fact that cats left as boarders in strange surroundings have been known to go on complete hunger strikes for nine days, without marked loss of condition.

Overall, the discerning cat lover has discovered that while his furry companion will agree to share his abode and be a most loving and devoted pet, he always retains a substantial degree of self-reliance and may at any time seek out a way of life elsewhere. While one may properly speak of the person who keeps a dog, as the dog's owner, the person who stands in the same relation to a cat may never truly be called the cat's owner. For the cat does not allow himself to be owned, but rather will agree for as long a time as is advantageous, either for food, shelter, or human companionship, to share your home. His behavior indicates that he considers the arrangement one of mutual respect and autonomy between peers.

Unlike dogs, cats seem more than able to exist on their own when they have been dispossessed or when they choose to leave the refinements and niceties of human society for more freedom. Once taken into your home, they adapt readily, but just as readily re-adapt to a lone existence.

If you are one who can appreciate the independence and individuality of an animal that seems to possess the awareness he was held sacred in ancient societies, associated with magic and witchcraft in others, performed the very useful and valuable function of ridding farms and homes of rats and other vermin, then you and the cat will get along fine. But if you expect an animal with an attitude bespeaking gratitude and dependence upon you for its every meal and eventual well being, that adopts an attitude of subservience and obedience, then you would do better looking elsewhere for a pet. For while the cat is capable of giving such homage, he will do so only when it is totally voluntary, and never when it is demanded.

Index

Index